Nothin' Goes Right the Night Before Christmas

Written by John Bell & Dan Bell

Illustrated by Charlie Layton

Based on the comedy of **RODNEY DANGERFIELD**

Special thanks to Joan Dangerfield

Copyright © 2021 by Paper Clip Productions, Inc.

All rights reserved. No part of this book may be reproduced
in any form without written permission.

Library of Congress Cataloging in Publication Number: 2021942086

ISBN: 978-1-7374955-0-5

Cover lettering by Risa Rodil
Design by Dan Bell, John Bell and Charlie Layton
Typeset in Recoleta

Published by Bell Brothers
Pitman, New Jersey

In memory of Rodney Dangerfield,
the man who got no respect.

'Twas the night before Christmas. Believe me, I checked.
Like every year prior, I'd get no respect.
My folks were so poor, we put lights on a stump,
In hopes that St. Nick would still visit this dump.

I was falling asleep, nestled snug in my bed,
When a thought from last Christmas popped into my head.

My friends got great presents, I felt so excluded.
All I got were batteries, toys not included.

In my letters to Santa, I begged and I pleaded.
My old dog was the worst. A new dog's what I needed.

When he'd bark at the door, I'd say, "Want to go out?"
No, he'd rather I left. What was that all about?

Then **crash!** From downstairs, there arose such a clatter.
Was it Santa or robbers? With my luck, the latter.

We get nothin' but break-ins, you don't understand.
Every window I close, I hit somebody's hand.

As I crept down the stairs, with each step came a creak.
Guess I shouldn't have snacked on those cookies all week.

I was chubby back then. Couldn't lose not a pound.
Tried to jog, but ran into each bakery I found.

And oh boy, was he plump. Many years past his prime.
When he steps on a scale, it says "one at a time".

He lay covered with gifts. Was this some kind of trick?
No. I knew at that moment, it must be St. Nick.

The strange hat on his head had thrown me for a loop.
Buy a hat like that, you get a free bowl of soup.

I stood there in awe at the gifts on the floor.
Then tore open each one, despite who they were for.

Why'd this kid get a BB gun? Cut me some slack.
All I got was a sweater, bull's eye on the back.

A doll house for Jane, and a toy truck for Pete.
A bat and a glove for the kid down the street.

I once got a bat. It was last Christmas day.
The first time I played with it, it flew away.

The last time I flew, I was far from delighted.
Southwest Airlines thanked me for flying United.

It was getting quite late, time to wake up St. Nick!
My mom's homemade cookies might just do the trick.

Santa's face turned pale green with one bite of his treat.
The way my mom cooks, we pray after we eat.

Santa spotted the gifts, all unwrapped in a pile.
"Get to wrappin' Rodney," he then said with a smile.

I always get caught. Oh, it just never ends.
One time at the bank, I got caught stealing pens.

As he filled all the stockings, I rewrapped each gift.
Then he slid me a present too heavy to lift,
"Not to spoil you, but here's one more gift from my sleigh."
I said, "Hey, I'm not spoiled! Lots of kids smell this way."

A dog sprang from the box, nearly knocking me over.
"C'mere Comet! No, Cupid! No... I'll name you Rover!"

My old dog, we named Egypt. My mom, how she'd fume,
When he'd leave little pyramids in every room.

"A dog's just what I wanted, but we need to chat.
How can I put this... That's the worst looking hat."

"It looks good on you though," I said, rolling my eyes.
Then I gave him my night cap, "Try this on for size."

Then St. Nick with his new hat, and I with my dog,
Made way to my chimney, which I feared he might clog.

And I heard him shout out, as he climbed up the flue,
"Look out for number one, but don't step in number two!"